S0-BFB-543

Schooltime Toppers
Creative Headers & Footers
for Classroom & Home

ISBN 1-59441-188-3

Contents

Credits

Illustrator: Dianne J. Hook
Project Director: Jennifer Weaver-Spencer
Content Design: Sherrill B. Flora, Jennifer Weaver-Spencer
Cover Production: Annette Hollister-Papp

Clip Art Assembly Basics

Here are some suggestions as you make your flyers,
announcements, or any project using clip art from this book.

Tools

Putting together the right tools will make your project go more smoothly and look better in the end. A good **copy machine** is a must. It's worth the extra effort to make sure your school or copy shop has machines that make clean copies. You will also need a bottle of white **paper correction fluid**, a fine-tip **black marker** to combine designs and add your own art to the project, **rubber cement** to mount the design onto your paper during the layout stage of your project, and **scissors** for cutting apart the designs you choose. Optional tools to help create a professional-looking project are a **nonreproducible blue pencil**, to make marks that will not show up on copies; a **proportion scale**, to help you determine the size of the reduction or enlargement necessary to fit your paper; and **blue grid paper** for laying out the project with straight lines.

Assembly Instructions for Creating a Page with a Lined Handwriting Template

1. Lined handwriting templates can be found on pages 4-6 of this book. Choose the template that is the most appropriate for the writing abilities of your students. Then, select a decorative border page.

2. Make copies of the lined handwriting template and border of your choice. Cut the lined handwriting template to fit inside the border. Use blue grid paper or a light table to make sure that you have properly centered the writing lines. Attach the template to the inside of the border with doublestick tape or rubber cement.

3. Try to keep a ¼-inch margin on all edges of your paper. If the cutting edges from the lined handwriting template are visible on your first copy, lighten the copy machine setting by one notch. Alternatively, use correction fluid on the first copy, and then use that copy to make the final journal pages for your students.

Hints

- Keep a ¼-inch margin on all edges of your paper.
- If the edges of the cutout pieces are visible on your copies, lighten the copy machine one notch or use correction fluid on one copy and then use it to make the final copies.
- Removable tape is great for creating layouts if you will be using the design more than once.

Journaling Templates on CD

Journal pages presented in black and white in this book are available in color on the enclosed CD. If desired, the images can be easily layered to create journal pages. The CD is Mac and PC compatible.

Have fun! You can become an artist and create wonderful
projects for your class with the help of this book!

Back to School

Welcome

Parents Needed

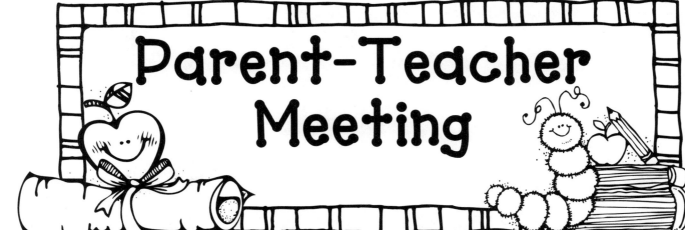

Parent-Teacher Meeting

Dear Parents...

Dear Students...

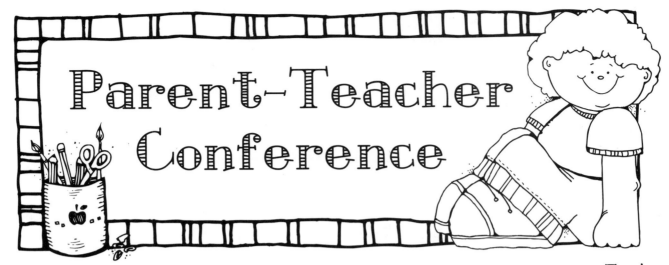

Parent-Teacher Conference

Teacher

MY TEACHER

Let You Know

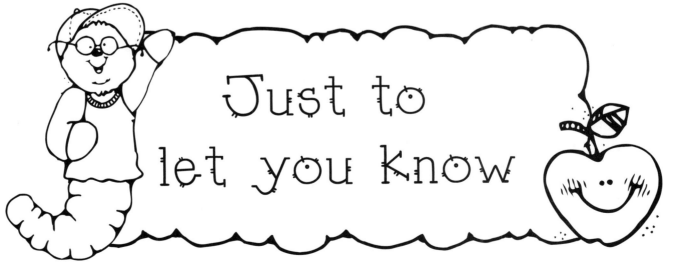

Just to let you know

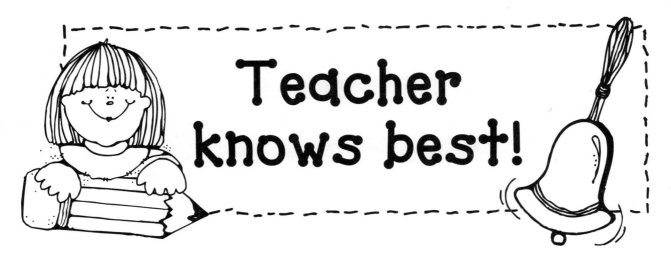

Teacher knows best!

Know the Rules

A Note from the Teacher

OUR CLASS IS THE BEST

CLASSMATES

Our Classroom Jobs

Supplies to Remember

Important Reminder

DON'T FORGET!

Daily Schedule

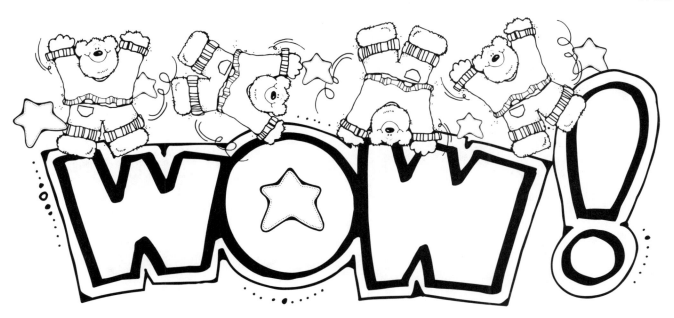

WOW!

Kindergarten News

First Grade News

Second Grade News

Third Grade News

Hall Pass

Phone Pass

Library Pass

Library Pass

Check Out

Library Check Out

Quiet

Shhh... Quiet Please

Boy Pass

Boy Pass

Girl Pass

Girl Pass

Appointment

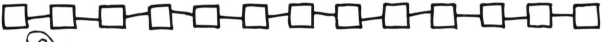

Schedule an appointment

Notice

Teacher Notice!

Important Reminder
to Everyone

For Boys
Only

Just for Girls

School Lunch

Special Coupon

_____

School Lunch Manners

Reading

MATH

Spelling

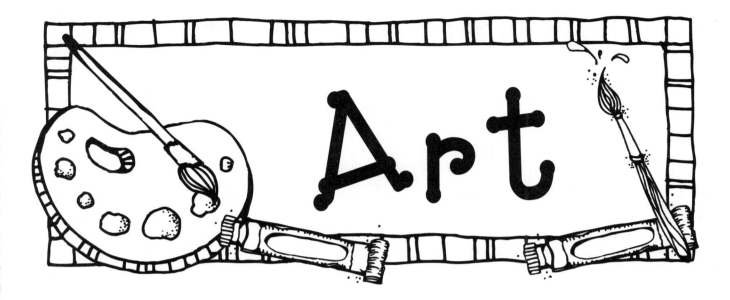

Progress Report

Here's the SCOOP

It's Time for a Change!

FIELD TRIP

Going

We're going to

Bus Trip

Hooray! It's Field Trip Time!

SCHOOL BUS

Free Time

Play

Time to Play!

Recess

Recess Rules

The latest "MOOs"

Just "paw-sing" to tell you

"Dog-gone" GREAT work!

Star Students

Shine

You Really Shine!

Good Work

Keep up the good work!

Your progress is out of this world!

Difference

You make a difference

Winner

You're a WINNER!

Excellent!

Terrific

Terrific!

yea! YOU

Totally Awesome!

Earn EXTRA Credit Points

Extra Credit

Try a Little Harder

A great big
THANK YOU

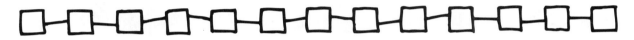

THANKS

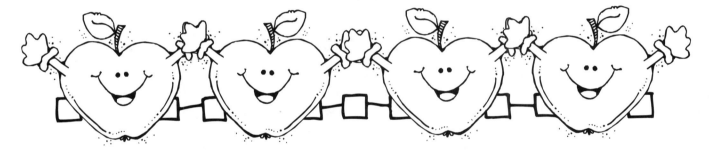

Thanks a bunch!

Birthday Time

Party Time!

Hooray! It's YOUR Birthday!

Happy Birthday   Happy Birthday   Happy Birthday

CeLeBRaTe!

It's YOUR special Day!

#1

Congratulations

Congrats

Congratulations
You deserve the best!

Treetops

Shout it from the treetops!

Hooray

Hooray!
YOU did it!

Volunteers Needed

School Help

Our school needs YOUR help!

Helping Hand

Lend a helping hand at school

EXTRA! EXTRA!
Read all about it!

Book Report Due

Library Books Due

Make a difference in Your community

Country

I love my COUNTRY

Love

Love where YOU Live!

Write

Write Every Day

Readers

Readers make the best writers

Homework

science
english
computers
math

Homework this week

Please bring a note from home.

Please Sign & Return

Note from home required!

Don't forget your note!

Please sign and return

Please sign and return

by this date:

Please sign and return

Please sign and return

Special Guest Today

Look who's HERE!

Hooray!

Special Visitor

It's Career Day!

Parents Welcome

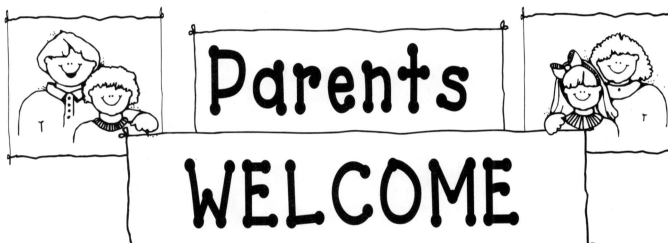

Parents WELCOME

Grow Up

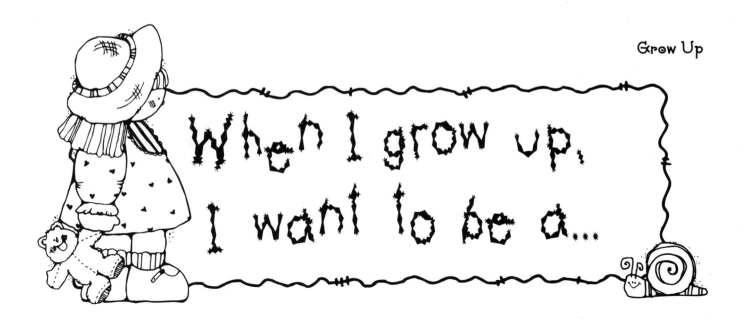

When I grow up, I want to be a...

My Graduation

GRADUATE

Graduation Day!

Happy New Year!

Bring in the New Year with a SMILE!

HOORAY! The New Year is Here!

44

Happy Valentine's Day

Our class Valentine's Party!

YEA! It's Valentine's Day!

Happy St. Patrick's Day!

May the luck of the Irish be with You!

It's YOUR Lucky Day!

Happy Easter

Happy Easter Wishes to YOU!

Here's "hoppin" your Spring Holiday is great!

National Teacher's Day!

Happy Mother's Day

Victoria Day!

Memorial Day!

Happy Father's Day!

First Day of Summer!

Vacation Time!

Happy Halloween

Boo to You!

Halloween Party

Halloween Party!

Frankly

"Frank"ly speaking...

Happy Thanksgiving

Give Thanks

Let's give Thanks

Thanksgiving

THANKSGIVING

Leaf Thanks

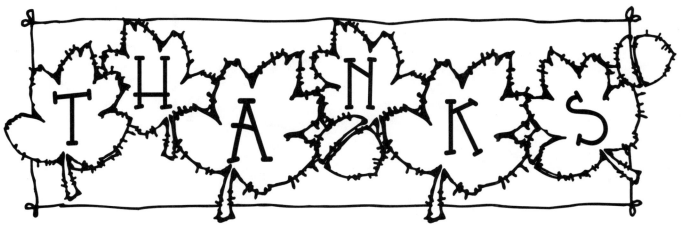

THANKS

Happy Holidays!

Holidays

HOLIDAYS

Greetings

Season's Greetings!

Christmas

Merry Christmas

Happy Kwanzaa

Happy Hanukkah

Hanukkah

HANUKKAH

Shalom

Basketball Schedule

Dance

Dance Schedule

Baseball

Baseball Schedule

Cheerleading Schedule

Time to Giddy-Up!

Fishin' Time!

Gone Campin'!

Golf

Great time to Golf!

Brrrr

Brrrr...
It's COLD out there!

Soccer Schedule

Score

Score!

Go Team

GO TEAM GO!

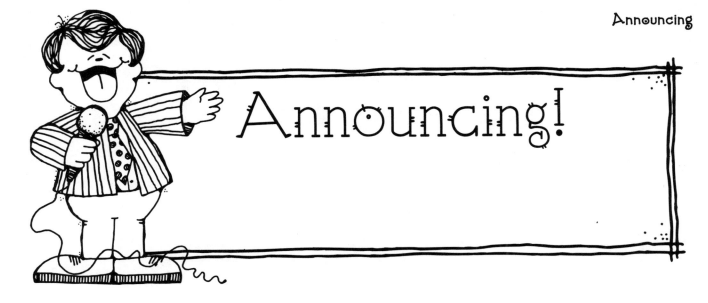

Announcing!

Worm Apple

Apples

Apple Bear

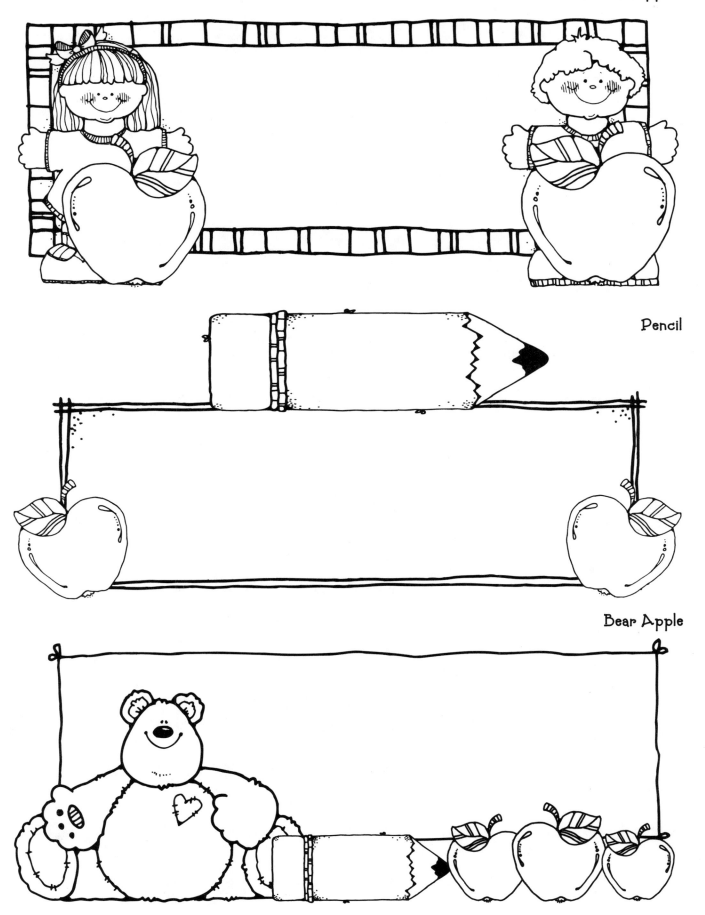

Pencil

Bear Apple

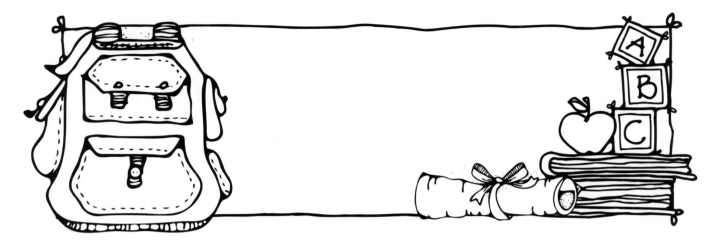

Love School

I L♥VE MY SCHOOL

Class

Pumpkins

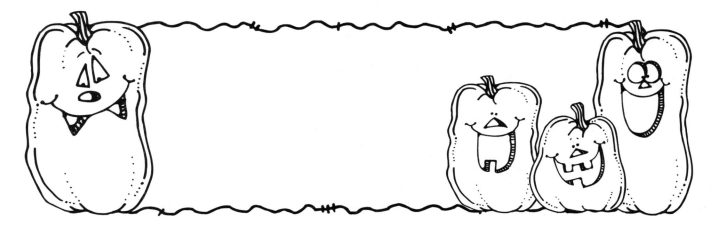

Mouse

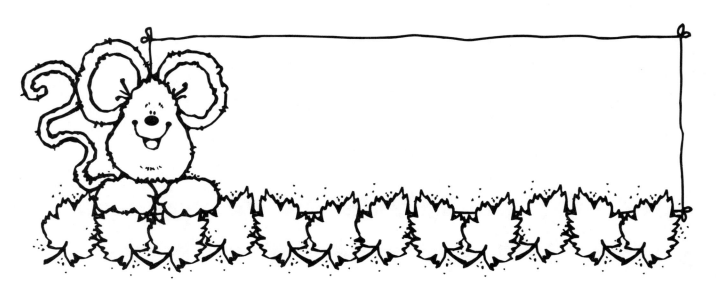

Bear Hats

Bear

Gifts

Bunnies

Flowers

Bee Hive